The Grand Design

THE PRINCE OF EGYPT

ADAPTED BY CATHERINE McCAFFERTY

TM & © 1998 DreamWorks

DreamWorks.

Published by Landoll, Inc.
Ashland, Ohio 44805

Moses was lost. He had run deep into the desert, far from his life as a Prince of Egypt. Around him, in every direction, he saw endless sand and scattered rocks. He did not know where  he was or which way to go. He knew only that he could not go back.

Moses pulled off his royal jewelry. The headpiece, gold necklace, gold cuffs, gold arm bands—all fell to the sand. Moses left them behind. Here in the desert, gold was nothing but a burden.

Back in the world of the palace, gold had meant everything. Moses had been raised as a Prince of Egypt, alongside Prince Rameses. But then Moses had learned that he had been born a Hebrew. He began to see how the Hebrew slaves suffered under the Egyptians' rule. In his heart, he began to feel their suffering.

One day, Moses tried to stop a guard from hurting a Hebrew slave. The guard fell from his scaffold and did not move again.

He had caused the guard's death! Frightened, Moses ran away.

Prince Rameses tried to stop Moses. But Moses knew that he could not return to his royal life. How could he pretend to be an Egyptian prince when he knew he was a Hebrew? With one last look at Rameses, Moses turned away. "Good-bye, brother."

Moses had fled so quickly that he had not even taken water with him. The fear he had felt at the guard's death was replaced by a new fear: Moses realized that he was truly alone. His throat burned for a drink of water, but there would be no palace servant or loving mother to bring it to him.

Moses scanned the desert. In the distance, he saw a dark shape. Clouds! They would bring rain! Instead of soothing rain, though, Moses felt a stinging wind. He fell to the ground in despair. A sandstorm

swirled around him, burying him right up to his hair.

Moses awoke to a sharp pain in his head. A camel was chewing on his hair as if it was the tastiest of grasses! Moses pushed the camel away. As he rubbed his sore scalp, he noticed a bag of water hanging from the camel's saddle. Moses grabbed hold of the bag, but before he could pull it loose, the camel started walking. Moses held onto the bag as the camel dragged him through the sand.

The camel did not stop until it came to a water trough. Moses ducked his head under the water and drank deeply. He did not even notice that he was sharing the trough with sheep. Never had water tasted so sweet! As Moses wiped his face, he heard a shout.

"Help! Let our sheep drink!" three young shepherd girls yelled, as several older shepherds tried to push the girls' sheep away.

The shepherds ignored the girls. Moses slipped over to their camels. "Aren't these your camels?" he called. When the shepherds turned to look, Moses sent the camels running. The shepherds ran off after them.

The rescue had taken the last of Moses' strength. He staggered to the nearby well and leaned heavily against it. But he lost his balance and fell into the well with a splash!

Moses could see only the silhouettes of the girls as they peered down at him. The bucket moved as they tried to pull him up. But it was no use. He was too heavy for them.

Then Moses heard a voice that sounded strangely familiar. "What are you girls doing?" a woman asked.

The girls answered, "We're trying to get the funny man out of the well."

"Well, that's one I've never heard before." The woman looked down the well. Moses heard her cry, "Oh, my! Don't worry, down there! We'll get you out! Hold on!"

As Moses reached the top of the well, he saw that the woman was Tzipporah. Moses had met her before, when she was a captive in the palace. He had helped her escape. But before that, Moses had backed Tzipporah into a pool of water. Moses hoped that Tzipporah would not remember that now.

But she did. "You!" Tzipporah exclaimed. She let go of the rope, and Moses splashed back into the well.

Moses heard one of the younger girls say, "That's why Papa says she'll never get married."

After a time, the sisters pulled Moses out of the well again. They led Moses to their settlement of Midian. A group of older Midianite women scrubbed Moses clean and gave him new clothes.

As Moses dressed, the leader of the Midianites burst into the tent. "Let me through! I want to see him!" He lifted Moses off the ground with a hearty hug. "You are most welcome, young man! You shall not be a stranger in this land! You have been sent to us as a blessing, and tonight, you shall be my honored guest!"

Moses stared as the Midianite leader hurried out.

Tzipporah smiled at Moses. "My father, Jethro—High Priest of Midian," she explained. She gathered her sisters and left the tent.

Moses wandered out through the settlement of tents that was Midian. He came to a large outdoor area where the Midianites were gathered. Everyone seemed to have a place.

Moses was not sure whether there was a place for him. Then one of Tzipporah's sisters spotted him and said, "Sit with me!"

"All right," Moses said. He realized how hungry he was and reached for a piece of fruit.

"Not yet!" the little girl whispered. She nodded toward the front of the area. Jethro had entered.

"My children," said Jethro, "let us give thanks for this bountiful food. And let us also give thanks for the presence of this brave young man whom we honor here tonight."

"Please, sir," said Moses, "I have done nothing in my life worth honoring."

Jethro looked puzzled. "First you rescued Tzipporah from Egypt. Then you defended my younger daughters at the well. You think that is nothing? It seems you do not know what is worthy of honor."

Jethro pulled a thread loose from the tapestry behind him. "One thread cannot see its place in the grand design," he said, motioning to the tapestry. "In the same way, Moses, you will not see your worth until you try to see your life through heaven's eyes."

Moses did not fully understand Jethro's words. But he felt the warmth of the Midianites' kindness. They did not have much food, but they were happy to share what they had with a stranger.

As the meal ended, the Midianites began to dance. Tzipporah's little sister tugged on his hand. "Dance with me," she said.

"No, no. I don't know how," Moses told her. As welcome as he felt, Moses was not yet ready to join the Midianites' dance.

In time, though, Moses joined the Midianites' life. As the years passed, he learned to be a shepherd. He came to know the shrubs that were signs of water in the desert. One day, as Moses led his sheep to a small spring, Jethro joined him.

"Look at them, Moses," Jethro said, pointing to the sheep. "You feel that you have nothing, that you are nothing. But to those sheep, you are everything. You mean more to them than the richest king, and that water means more to them than a king's gold."

Moses thought about Jethro's words as he brought the sheep back that night. He had led them to water, such a simple thing. But to the sheep, water meant life. In the desert, God had led him to the well near Midian—and to a new life. The Midianites had given him the simple gifts of food, shelter, clothing. With those gifts came something far greater. The Midianites had given him a home.

Living among the Midianites, Moses had lost his princely habit of selfishness. He had grown to love the people of Midian. In a very special way, Moses had grown to love Tzipporah. With his love for her, Moses forgot to think of himself. He thought only of what would bring Tzipporah happiness.

Moses asked Tzipporah to marry him. All of Midian danced with joy as Jethro blessed the new couple.

"Dance with me," Tzipporah said to Moses.

This time, Moses gladly joined the dance.

Each new day, Moses marveled at the peace and happiness that he had found in Midian. Never as a prince of Egypt, with all his riches, had he felt so content. It seemed he had found his place in the grand design—by Tzipporah's side.

One morning, as Moses searched for a lost sheep, he came upon a bush in flames. Moses paused and stared. The flames burned, but the bush remained whole and uncharred. Moses put his staff into the flames. It did not burn.

"Moses...Moses," a voice called.

"Who are you?" Moses did not see anyone nearby. He held his staff before him.

"I am the God of your ancestors, Abraham, Isaac, Jacob, Sarah, Rebecca, Rachel, and Leah," the voice answered. "Take the sandals from your feet, for you stand on holy ground."

Moses took off his sandals. "What do you want with me?"

"I have come down to deliver my people out of slavery and bring them out of Egypt. So unto Pharaoh I shall send you," God spoke to him.

Moses shrank from the bush. "Me? Who am I to lead these people? They'll never believe me."

"I shall be with you," God told him.

"But I was their enemy!" Moses protested. "You've chosen the wrong messenger. How can I even speak to these people?"

An angry wind whipped at Moses' robe. The fire in the bush grew brighter still. Moses put his hands before his face, afraid to look at the flames. Then the wind calmed, and drew Moses closer to the bush.

"Oh, Moses, I shall be with you when you go to the king of Egypt. But Pharaoh will not listen. So I will stretch out my hand and smite Egypt with all my wonders. Take the staff in your hand. With it you shall do my wonders. I shall be with you, Moses."

The flames faded from the bush. God had spoken. And as God had spoken, God had shown Moses the slavery of his people. Moses took his staff in hand. He would meet with the Pharaoh. It was time to prepare for his journey to Egypt.

Moses hurried back to Midian. He told Tzipporah what God had commanded him to do.

"But Moses," said Tzipporah, "you're just one man."

Moses motioned to the Midianites going about their lives outside. "Tzipporah, please . . . look at your family. They are free. They have hopes and dreams and a promise of a life with dignity. That is what I want for my people. And that is why I must do the task that God has given me."

Tzipporah watched her family outside. She loved them with all her heart, and wanted only their happiness. Then she understood the feeling Moses had for the Hebrews. Tzipporah turned to her husband and hugged him. "I'm going with you."

They left for Egypt with the blessing of Jethro and the prayers of the Midianites. Their journey took them across the desert where Moses, rich in gold, had been lost so many years before. This time, rich in faith and love, Moses knew his way. He had found his true place in the grand design.